INNER CRITIC
— VS —
INNER WARRIOR

UNLEASH YOUR TRUE POWER BY LEARNING TO BALANCE SELF-DOUBT AND SELF-BELIEF

DONOVAN GARETT

Copyright © 2025 AlgoRhythms Studios, Ltd. All rights reserved.

Any attempt to reproduce, translate and/or distribute in any form any part of this work beyond that permitted by Section 107 or 108 of the 1976 United States Copyright Act without express written consent by the copyright owner is illegal. No part of this publication may be duplicated, stored in a retrieval system, or transmitted in any form or by any means electronic, mechanical, photocopied, recorded or otherwise, without the prior written permission of the publisher. Requests for permission or further information can be sent by U.S. mail at the following address:

AlgoRhythms Studios, Ltd.

P.O. BOX 35643

Cleveland, Ohio 44135

United States of America

DISCLAIMER. This publication is intended (but not guaranteed) to provide accurate information in regard to the subject matter covered. Some information may not be applicable to every reader or every situation. It is sold with the understanding that neither the author, publisher, nor any other person or entity connected with the creation, publication, or distribution of this publication provides legal, accounting, medical, or other professional services. If expert assistance is required, the services of a competent professional should be sought.

PRINT ISBN: 978-1-963267-30-3

E-BOOK ISBN: 978-1-963267-31-0

Library of Congress Control Number: 2025901365

Printed in the United States of America

Dedicated to everyone forced to be strong before their time.

"I take pleasure in weakness... For as soon as I am weak then I am powerful."
— 2 Corinthians 12:10

Contents

1. Say 'What'? . . .   1
2. Meet Your Inner Critic   5
   Who, Exactly, is My Inner Critic?
   How Our Inner Critic Traps Us
   Developing Self-Awareness
   Get Ready to Face Your Inner Critic
3. The Impact of Self-Doubt   19
   Understanding Self-Doubt
   The Connection Between Fear and Self-Doubt
   Recognizing Self-Doubt in Your Life
   Challenging Negative Thought Patterns
   From Self-Doubt to Self-Belief
4. Awakening Your Inner Warrior   33
   Meet Your Inner Warrior
   Build a Relationship with Your Inner Warrior
   Your Inner Warrior in Action:
   Facing Tough Decisions and Challenges

Sustaining Your Inner Warrior
The Connection Between Self-Belief
and Your Inner Warrior

5. Overcoming Limiting Beliefs   51
   What is Self-Belief?
   Identify and Reframe Limiting Beliefs
   Build Confidence by Taking Action
   Anticipate and Manage Setbacks

6. Balancing Your Inner Critic and Inner Warrior   65
   Achieving Inner Balance
   Recognize When Your Inner Critic is Taking Over
   Managing Your Inner Critic
   Strengthening Your Inner Warrior
   Making Your Inner Critic and Inner Warrior
   Work Together Harmoniously
   Continuous Learning and Intentionality

7. Building Courage and Resilience   79
   The Interplay Between Courage and Resilience
   Building Resilience Despite Challenges
   Strengthening Resilience Over Time
   Why Vulnerability is
   One of Your Greatest Strengths

The Path to Self-Mastery

8. The Journey Toward Self-Mastery   91
   The 3 Pillars of Self-Mastery
   Self-Awareness and Self-Mastery
   Developing Self-Discipline
   The Role of Self-Compassion in Self-Mastery
   Reflecting on Your Growth and Progress
   Embracing Self-Mastery as a Lifelong Process
   Own Your Power. Shape Your Destiny.

Where to Find Help   109
   United States
   Canada
   United Kingdom
   Mexico

Let's Connect!   115

Love FREE Books?   117

Chapter 1
Say 'What'? . . .
Why This Book Almost Never Existed

Are you KIDDING ME?!?! . . . It'll never work.

Do you know how absurd that sounds?

. . . And besides, don't you know how much competition there is out there? . . . All by people much smarter, and more talented than you are.

It'll fail.

You'll fail . . . just like you always do.

Just give up now before you *really* embarrass yourself.

"Say 'what'?!?! . . ."

What you're hearing are not the words of a cruel, heartless, verbal abuser.

Well, maybe you are . . .

It was the voice of my Inner Critic when I decided to begin writing. Despite having experience writing everything from complex

1

engineering manuals and technical schematics to legal briefs, I felt wholly inadequate to begin writing my first book.

At first.

After spending several weeks pondering both my failures and successes, I decided to take action despite the voice of my inner critic. I realized that the more action I took toward reaching my goal, the less vocal the Inner Critic became.

Eventually, the voice of my Inner Critic gave way to the voice of my Inner Warrior—encouraging me to continue, reassuring me that success is not always measured by gross sales, profit margin, or the other traditional benchmarks that we've been conditioned to accept which ultimately define our success.

No.

At its core, true success means pushing forward toward your long-term goals despite fear, uncertainty or doubt.

It means being willing to confront failure, accept the lessons it teaches us, and move on.

Whether we like to admit it or not, we all have two voices chattering incessantly within our minds: one that holds us back, and another that pushes us forward. Unfortunately, for most, the voice holding them back often wins. It prevents them from even trying to move past their comfort zone and into the realm of growth.

Personally, I've used many of the techniques in this book to move past fears, embrace growth, and continually progress toward self-mastery.

Admittedly, I am very much still a work in progress. But the point is that we all have to start somewhere. So, it is my sincere hope that this book will help you move closer to your goals and inspire you on a similar path.

I'm thrilled and honored to be a part of your journey.

Let's get started.

Chapter 2
Meet Your Inner Critic

"You have been criticizing yourself for years and it hasn't worked. Try approving of yourself and see what happens."

Louise Hay

Let's start by taking a deep breath. Take a moment to reflect on your past. Were you relentlessly criticized, insulted or even bullied during your childhood?

I was.

The brutal truth is that our past life experiences create our present reality—including the tendency to amplify the voice of our Inner Critic. More often than not, this process occurs without us even realizing it.

In this chapter, we'll explore the dark origins of our Inner Critic and how it is shaped by past experiences and learned behaviors. We'll discuss how it can both protect and limit us and how it often surfaces through negative self-talk and self-doubt.

But first, let's identify our Inner Critic.

Who, Exactly, is My Inner Critic?

Our Inner Critic is an internal voice that constantly judges, critiques, and undermines our confidence. This internal voice continuously operates in the background of our minds, reminding us of our flaws, mistakes, and shortcomings. It acts as a harsh judge, holding us back from reaching our full potential.

Our Inner Critic is a never-ending self-commentator, finding fault in every action and decision we make and casting doubt on our abilities and worth. Whether it's telling us that we're not smart enough, not attractive enough, or not capable enough, the Inner Critic thrives on feeding our insecurities and planting seeds of self-doubt in our minds.

Although the dialogue varies from person to person, the voice itself is not unique. Everyone has an Inner Critic. For some, it may be a loud, ever-present force that heavily influences daily life, while for others, it might be a quieter voice that surfaces only in specific situations.

Your Inner Critic can take on many forms and tones, but its impact is universally felt. It can prevent you from taking risks, stifle your creativity, and keep you stuck by fear, doubt and hesitation.

Where Does Your Inner Critic Come From?

Our Inner Critic forms in early childhood, deeply influenced by the feedback and interactions we receive from those around us. Sadly, experiences such as bullying, verbal or physical abuse, harsh criticism, and other similar experiences allow the Inner Critic to flourish in our minds.

Parents play the most significant role in shaping this internal voice. Despite having the best of intentions, parents can sometimes be overly critical or set unrealistically high standards. As a result, as children, we internalize these attitudes, leading to a persistent, self-critical inner dialogue.

Our academic experiences also contribute to the Inner Critic's voice. Bullies, cliques, and relentless pressure to succeed academically, fit in socially, or meet teachers' expectations can reinforce feelings of inadequacy and self-judgment.

In particular, the methods that schools use to punish mistakes and promote rigid, outdated grading standards further erode self-confidence, creative thinking, and a willingness to take risks. Social interactions with peers or authority figures further mold our self-perception, instilling a fear of rejection or failure that can last for decades.

Cultural and societal standards also play a substantial role in this process. Society can impose high (often unreachable) expectations regarding success, appearance, and behavior. These standards are reinforced through social media, cultural narratives, and social norms and further amplified by mainstream media. These influences create an unrealistic image of perfection that we feel compelled to aspire to.

As we strive to meet these external expectations, our Inner Critic becomes increasingly vocal, comparing us unfavorably to others and then criticizing us for falling short. This pervasive sense of not being *"good enough"* directly results from trying to align our self-worth with external benchmarks rather than our internal values.

The Psychological Roots of the Inner Critic

Our Inner Critic can also be understood in psychological terms. Although now largely viewed as obsolete by modern psychologists, Sigmund Freud's concept of the superego provides an explanation. According to Freud, the superego acts as the moral conscience within our psyche, echoing the critical and judgmental voices of 'authority figures' from our early upbringing. It strives for perfection and can be overly harsh, leading to feelings of guilt and inadequacy. [1]

---

1. See, e.g., Anna K. Schaffner, PH.D, Living With Your Inner Critic https ://www.annakschaffner.com/post/living-with-your-inner-critic

Cognitive-behavioral models offer another perspective, suggesting that the Inner Critic is a form of negative self-talk developed through repeated patterns of thinking. These patterns are established in response to negative experiences or learned behaviors and become automatic over time. This constant barrage of self-criticism undermines our self-esteem and limits our ability to see our strengths as others do. [2]

The Inner Critic's Role in Our Lives

The Inner Critic is a complex part of our psyche that serves a dual purpose. On one hand, it can highlight areas where we can improve, encouraging self-reflection and growth. This voice often serves as a motivator, pushing us to strive for higher standards and to avoid repeating past mistakes. In this way, our Inner Critic can be a valuable tool for self-awareness and self-improvement, helping us to learn and refine our skills over time.

However, more often than not, this voice quickly becomes excessively harsh and counterproductive. Instead of offering constructive feedback, our Inner Critic takes on the role of a relentless judge, constantly pointing out our perceived flaws and shortcomings. It make us feel inadequate, regardless of our past achievements.

---

2. See, e.g., Cognitive Behavioral Therapy Los Angeles, CBT for Low Self-Esteem, https://cogbtherapy.com/cbt-for-improving-low-confidence

This excessive self-criticism prevents us from taking risks and stepping out of our comfort zones. We might avoid new challenges or opportunities because we fear failure or judgment, holding us back from reaching our full potential. When the Inner Critic dominates our thoughts, it stifles creativity, limits our personal growth, and keeps us trapped in a perpetual cycle of fear and self-doubt.

Identifying the Inner Critic's Voice

To manage our Inner Critic, we must learn to recognize its voice and understand how it operates. The voice of our Inner Critic generally sounds like an internal monologue filled with negative and judgmental statements. Common phrases might include: *"You're not good enough," "You'll never succeed," "Why did you even try?"* and *"Everyone else is better than you."* These statements typically sound absolute and harsh, leaving little room for nuance or self-compassion. They focus on what went wrong with laser-like precision, magnifying our mistakes, and minimizing our achievements.

The rhetoric of the Inner Critic is repetitive, following familiar scripts that play over and over in our minds like a broken record. This voice can be instantly triggered by criticism, temporary setbacks or failures, or even by comparing ourselves to others. It thrives in moments of vulnerability, turning our insecurities against us.

Reflecting on personal experiences can help identify when our Inner Critic has been particularly vocal. Think back to times when you felt discouraged or anxious. What was your inner dialogue like in those moments? Recognizing these patterns is the first step towards challenging and changing them.

How Our Inner Critic Traps Us

Our Inner Critic uses several tactics to keep us in a perpetual state of self-doubt. One of the most common is perfectionism. In our minds, we often set impossibly high standards for ourselves, convinced that anything less than a perfect outcome is equivalent to total failure.

This uncompromising pursuit of perfection can lead to stress, burnout, and a constant feeling of inadequacy, as we can never actually live up to these unrealistic expectations. Perfectionism keeps us from recognizing our achievements, no matter how significant, and instead focuses on what should have been done better.

Another common tactic is ***constant comparison*** with others. In a world filled with pre-defined standards of seemingly perfect lives thanks to social media, advertising, and pop culture, we are tempted to measure our worth against that of others, highlighting just how far we fall short.

Whether it's comparing our careers, relationships, or personal achievements, this promotes intense feelings of envy, jealousy, and self-doubt. We start to believe that we are not as capable or successful as those around us, which further diminishes our confidence and prevents us from appreciating our unique strengths and accomplishments.

Catastrophizing is another common tactic. This involves blowing minor setbacks or mistakes out of proportion and always imagining the worst possible outcome. Focusing on exaggerated fears creates a sense of anxiety and hopelessness, making it difficult to take positive action or see situations objectively.

Our Inner Critic also plays a significant role in developing ***imposter syndrome***. Imposter syndrome is a persistent belief that our success is undeserved and that, despite evidence to the contrary, we are not as competent or capable as others perceive us to be.

When we suffer from imposter syndrome, we become convinced that our achievements result from luck or chance rather than our innate abilities and hard work. This, in turn, creates a constant fear of being exposed as a fraud, leading to chronic self-doubt and anxiety despite having clear and tangible evidence of our accomplishments.

The Traps of Self-Criticism

The Inner Critic's tactics are effective because they lure us into traps of self-criticism that distort our internal perception of ourselves and our capabilities. One such trap is **overgeneralization**. This means drawing broad, negative conclusions from a single event or limited experience.

For instance, after a single setback or mistake, our Inner Critic might convince us that we are failures, disregarding all occurences of past success. This often makes it a challenge to view situations objectively and negatively impacts our self-esteem.

Another trap is **emotional reasoning**, where we believe something *must be true* simply because it *feels true*. If we feel inadequate or insecure, the Inner Critic tells us that we must not be good enough, despite facts to the contrary. Emotional reasoning ignores logic and reality, allowing the Inner Critic to continuously reinforce a negative self-image based solely on emotion.

These traps reinforce a pattern of self-doubt and prevent personal growth. When we fall into these traps, we limit our ability to see ourselves and our lives rationally. We become part of a negative narrative that hinders our progress and keeps us from recognizing our true potential. Overcoming these traps requires a conscious effort to challenge these distorted thoughts and replace them with more balanced, constructive beliefs.

Developing Self-Awareness

Recognizing the Inner Critic's voice is the first step toward reducing its impact on your life. Start with self-reflection exercises that bring awareness to when and how this voice shows up. Reflect on recent experiences where you felt judged or criticized by your inner voice. Ask yourself: *"What triggered these feelings?" "Was there a specific event, interaction, or thought that sparked this self-criticism?" "What are the exact words or phrases my Inner Critic uses?"*

Journaling can help with this process. Note the times when you felt your Inner Critic was particularly vocal. Describe the situation, thoughts, and feelings in as much detail as possible. As you document these experiences, look for common patterns or triggers. *Do certain places, situations or people tend to bring out your Inner Critic more than others? Are there recurring themes in the criticisms you hear?* By identifying these patterns, you can begin to anticipate when your Inner Critic might appear and prepare to silence it if necessary.

In addition to self-reflection, work on developing self-awareness using mindfulness practices. Mindfulness involves paying attention to the present moment without judgment. When you feel that familiar pang of self-doubt, or hear that critical voice in your head, pause and acknowledge it. Remember that this is your Inner Critic speaking, not a reflection of your true self or abilities.

Another useful technique is cognitive awareness, which involves actively monitoring your thoughts and questioning their validity. When you catch yourself engaging in negative self-talk, pause and ask yourself: *"Are these thoughts are based on facts or assumptions?"* Challenge your Inner Critic by focusing on evidence that contradicts its negativity.

It's also important to distinguish between constructive self-reflection and destructive self-criticism. Constructive self-reflection helps you learn and grow by evaluating your actions and identifying areas for improvement in a balanced and compassionate way.

On the other hand, destructive self-criticism focuses on perceived flaws and shortcomings, exaggerating them and causing unnecessary harm to your self-esteem. Awareness helps you to differentiate between these two forms of inner dialogue and choose a more constructive path forward. Developing this level of awareness takes practice and patience, but over time, it can significantly reduce the Inner Critic's power over your life.

Get Ready to Face Your Inner Critic

Before confronting your Inner Critic, acknowledge the impact it has had on your life. Consider how this critical voice has influenced your decisions and shaped your experiences. Perhaps you missed valuable opportunities because you doubted your abilities or feared failure.

Or, maybe your relationships are strained by being overly sensitive to criticism or defensive when receiving feedback. Our Inner Critic frequently undermines our self-esteem, making us feel unworthy or incapable of success, leading to a vicious cycle of negative thinking and self-sabotage.

Recognizing this influence is an important step in reclaiming your power. You slowly begin to separate yourself from this negative voice. This increased self-awareness allows you to see your Inner Critic for what it is—a part of you, but not the entirety of who you are. The Inner Critic's allegations not a reflection of your true potential or capabilities but rather a learned pattern of thinking that can be changed.

Preparing for Life-Altering Change

After acknowledging the Inner Critic's impact, it's time to prepare for change. Your Inner Critic may have been a constant companion in your life, but it does not have to define your future. You have the power to transform this voice and reshape your internal narrative. While it might seem daunting at first, remember that every step you take towards understanding and challenging your Inner Critic is a step towards a more confident, empowered version of yourself.

Change begins with a commitment to yourself. Recognize that you deserve better. You deserve to live without the constant burden of self-doubt and harsh judgment. By cultivating a more balanced and compassionate inner dialogue, you open the door to growth, self-acceptance, and true empowerment. This process is about more than just quieting the Inner Critic—it's about awakening your Inner Warrior.

As we will discuss throughout the book, your Inner Warrior represents the strength, courage, and resilience within you. It's the part of you that knows your worth, believes in your abilities, and is ready to conquer challenges head-on.

In the next chapter, we will dive deeper into how self-doubt manifests, the fears that fuel it, and the long-term consequences it can have on your actions and decisions. We will also begin the process of transforming self-criticism into self-empowerment, exploring practical ways to help you build a stronger, more resilient mindset.

Chapter 3
The Impact of Self-Doubt

"Doubt kills more dreams than failure ever will."
                                            Suzy Kassem

Self-doubt can shape your life in powerful ways. It creeps into your thoughts, questions your abilities, and holds you back from fully pursuing your dreams. Unlike the Inner Critic, which generally targets specific actions that you want to take, or qualities that you want to cultivate, self-doubt casts a much wider net, affecting how you view yourself as a whole.

It quietly whispers that you're not capable enough, not worthy enough, and that you're bound to fail if you try something new. This invasive sense of inadequacy can limit your potential, keeping you fearful and hesitant to make real changes.

In this chapter, we'll explore how self-doubt manifests in daily life and how it can influence our decisions, behaviors, and overall well-being. You'll see the relationship between self-doubt and fear, and how fear of failure, rejection or the unknown fuels this negative mindset.

Understanding Self-Doubt

Self-doubt is a persistent feeling of uncertainty about our abilities, worth, and the quality of our decisions. It pops up when we least expect it, from second-guessing life choices to feeling paralyzed when faced with new challenges. Self-doubt causes us to question our competence, worry excessively about mistakes even before they're made, and cause us to fear that we're not good enough to succeed. Over time, this lack of confidence becomes evident in every aspect of life, from personal relationships to our career choices, creating a seemingly insurmountable barrier to reaching our full potential.

Our Inner Critic and self-doubt are closely linked. While our Inner Critic is the voice that actively tries to undermine our confidence by highlighting perceived flaws and past mistakes, self-doubt is the byproduct of these statements. Self-doubt occurs as an emotional response to the voice of our Inner Critic. In other words, our Inner Critic sows the seeds of doubt, and self-doubt is what is harvested. Together, they form a powerful cycle of negative thinking that is difficult to break, reinforcing a mindset that limits our opportunities for long-term growth, fulfillment and happiness.

The Universality of Self-Doubt

Self-doubt is a universal experience. All of us, regardless of age, race, status, or level of success, encounter self-doubt at some point in our life. It doesn't discriminate based on achievements or external appearances. People who seem outwardly confident, accomplished and polished struggle with feelings of inadequacy and uncertainty. This is a reminder that self-doubt is a natural part of being human.

Understanding the commonality of self-doubt can help reduce the shame and isolation that you might feel when it occurs. Acknowledging these simple truths will help you to see self-doubt as a common challenge that everyone faces—not a personal flaw. This is a crucial step in learning to manage self-doubt.

'Ripple Effects' of Self-Doubt

Self-doubt has a tendency to impact our lives in ways that we often don't even recognize. It doesn't just impact how we feel about ourselves—it can harm our personal relationships, career choices and overall personal growth.

For instance, in relationships, self-doubt can manifest as insecurity, making it difficult to trust others or believe that we are worthy of love and respect. This can lead to *"clinginess,"* jealousy, or withdrawal, creating added tension and eroding intimacy.

At work, we might avoid new opportunities to prove ourselves, or hesitate to openly voice our ideas. It can make us feel less capable than our colleagues who do similar work, resulting in an unwillingness to seek a promotion or take on additional responsibilities. This, in turn, can keep us professionally stagnant.

Our personal growth can also be stunted by self-doubt. When we constantly question our abilities and fear failure, we stop taking the necessary risks that lead to personal growth. We don't allow ourselves to be challenged, step outside of our comfort zone or set ambitious goals because we're afraid of not measuring up to our internal definition of *"success."*

Self-doubt can be infectious, spreading from one area of life to another. For example, doubts about our professional ability can affect self-esteem in social situations, leading to a broader sense of inadequacy. This shows that self-doubt doesn't occur in isolation. It can subtly permeate all areas of life, creating a cycle of negativity that is difficult to break free from.

Self-Doubt's Psychological and Emotional Toll

The psychological effects of self-doubt are far-reaching. Constantly doubting your worth and abilities can lead to anxiety, where you're constantly worried about making mistakes or being judged by others. This heightened state of worry can make everyday interactions and decisions feel overwhelming, sapping your energy and focus.

Over time, chronic self-doubt can contribute to anxiety and depression, as feelings of inadequacy and hopelessness take root. You may begin to believe that you are incapable of any amount of change or self-improvement, leading to a feeling of despair.

Self-doubt also erodes self-esteem. When you repeatedly question your abilities and second-guess your decisions, it reinforces the belief that you are not good enough to face new challenges. This lack of confidence affects how you present yourself to the world and how you perceive your value. Low self-esteem can create a self-fulfilling prophecy where you avoid opportunities for fear of failure, thereby limiting your experiences and reinforcing the belief that you are not capable.

The emotional toll of self-doubt is equally significant. Living with constant self-criticism can make you feel like you're always under attack, even if the attack is coming from within. This can lead to a volatile mix of frustration, anger, and sadness, as you struggle to reconcile your perceived shortcomings with your desire for success and happiness. Overall, the weight of these emotions can be exhausting, leaving you feeling drained and unmotivated.

The Connection Between Fear and Self-Doubt

Fear is at the heart of self-doubt. It's a powerful emotion that shapes our view of both ourselves and the world around us. Thus, *fear of failure* is one of the most common fears that feeds into self-doubt. When we're afraid of not succeeding, we start to question our abilities and whether we're capable of achieving our goals. This makes us hesitant to try new things or take on challenges, leading to a cycle of self-doubt where we convince ourselves that we're not capable or worthy of success.

Another significant contributor to self-doubt is the ***fear of rejection***. This often stems from a desire for acceptance and approval from others. When we fear being judged or criticized, we worry that we're not good enough to meet the expectations of others. This can cause us to avoid situations where we might face intense scrutiny or disapproval from our peers, colleagues or loved ones.

Finally, ***fear of the unknown*** plays a critical role in self-doubt. When we don't know what to expect, we often imagine the worst-case scenario. This fear of uncertainty can prevent us from stepping out of our comfort zone or exploring new opportunities, as we become overly concerned about the risks and challenges we might face, ignoring the potential benefits. All these fears combine to create a fertile ground for self-doubt to grow, undermining our confidence and limiting our potential.

The Paralyzing Effect of Fear

Fear-induced self-doubt can have a paralyzing effect on our lives. When we're consumed by fear, we become hesitant, making it difficult to take decisive action or move forward from one goal to another. This paralysis can prevent us from seizing opportunities that can lead to growth and success. Instead of taking risks and embracing challenges, we become stuck in a state of inaction, unable to overcome the fear that holds us back.

This state of *"analysis paralysis"* is often reinforced by a constant stream of negative thoughts and *'what-if'* scenarios. We tend to look for potential failure points rather than possibilities for success. This focus on fear and doubt creates a mental barrier that prevents us from seeing our strengths and capabilities, making it even more difficult to believe in ourselves and our ability to overcome challenges.

The paralyzing effect of fear can also lead to **avoidance behaviors**, where we actively avoid situations or opportunities that might trigger our deep-seated fears. This avoidance only strengthens our self-doubt, as we never give ourselves the chance to prove our fears wrong or build confidence in our abilities. Over time, this pattern of fear and avoidance can significantly limit our potential, keeping us from achieving personal fulfillment.

Recognizing Self-Doubt in Your Life

Self-doubt most commonly arises from specific triggers—situations or experiences that cause you to question your abilities and worth. One of the most common of these is criticism, especially from close family and friends. When your actions, appearance, or decisions, are criticized, it can shake your confidence and make you question your value. This is especially true if the criticism comes from someone whose opinion you hold in high regard. The sting of criticism can linger long after the statements are made, allowing self-doubt to take root and grow.

Another trigger for self-doubt might be comparison with others. Today, social media and constant connectivity gives us a peek into others' lives. Thus, it's easy to fall into the trap of comparing ourselves to them. When you see friends, coworkers or strangers achieving milestones, enjoying successes, or living what seems like perfect lives, you might start to feel inadequate or believe that you're not measuring up. This comparison can erode your self-esteem and amplify negative feelings about your own abilities and accomplishments.

Our past failures can also play a role in triggering self-doubt. When we experience setbacks or failures, those memories can linger, causing us to doubt our ability to succeed in the future. We might worry that *"history will repeat itself"* or that we're not capable of overcoming the challenges ahead. This might create a fear of trying new things, because we become hyper-focused on avoiding failure rather than pursuing growth.

It's important to reflect on your experiences and identify your own self-doubt triggers. Consider situations where you most often feel insecure or unsure of yourself. Are there specific people, places, or events that tend to provoke these feelings? By pinpointing the triggers that activate your self-doubt, you can take proactive steps to manage it.

'Red Flags' That Indicate Self-Doubt

In addition to the triggers that are more obscure, there are also self-doubt *'red flags'* that are somewhat easier to identify. Procrastination is one of the most common red flags of self-doubt. When you doubt your ability to succeed, you might put off ambitious tasks or projects, fearing that the outcome will not measure up to your standards. This pattern of avoidance behavior can keep you stuck in a cycle of inaction and uncertainty.

Another red flag is outright avoidance of challenges. If you frequently shy away from new opportunities or avoid new responsibilities that push you outside of your comfort zone, it could be a sign that self-doubt is holding you back. You might see challenges as threats to your self-esteem, prompting you to avoid them altogether.

Do you know someone who constantly puts themselves down? **Excessive self-criticism** is another common indicator of self-doubt. When we berate ourselves for our perceived flaws or downplay our achievements, it's a clear sign that self-doubt is influencing self-perception. Relentless self-criticism can erode our confidence, and prevents us from recognizing our strengths and success.

Here are some questions for self-reflection:

- *Do I frequently compare myself to others and feel inadequate as a result?*

- *Do I avoid taking on new challenges or responsibilities because I fear failure?*

- *Do I often procrastinate, especially if it requires me to step outside my comfort zone?*

- *Do I constantly criticize my abilities, appearance, or decisions, even when others provide positive feedback?*

These questions can help you identify patterns of self-doubt. By recognizing these red flags, you can start to challenge self-doubt and replace it with more constructive and empowering thoughts.

Challenging Negative Thought Patterns

One of the best ways to break the cycle of self-doubt is to challenge the negative thought patterns that fuel it. Cognitive-behavioral techniques are particularly useful for identifying and reshaping these patterns.

The first step in this process is becoming aware of your thoughts and recognizing when they are negative or self-defeating. Pay attention to the internal dialogue that occurs when you face a challenge or experience a setback. *Are your thoughts filled with doubt, fear, or self-criticism? Do you find yourself predicting future failures or assuming the worst possible outcome?*

Once you've identified these negative thought patterns, the next step is to challenge them. Ask yourself whether these thoughts are based on facts, assumptions, or fears. Weigh the evidence for and against these thoughts. *Are there concrete reasons to believe you will fail, or are you overgeneralizing based on a single negative experience?* By critically evaluating your thoughts, you can begin to see them for what they are—distorted reflections of your fears rather than accurate assessments of reality.

To help reframe these thoughts, try the following exercises:

Record Your Thoughts: Write down a specific situation that triggered self-doubt and the negative thoughts and emotions that arose. Then, challenge these thoughts by listing concrete evidence against them. Finally, reframe the negative thoughts into more balanced, realistic, and positive statements. For example, instead of thinking, *"I always mess up,"* you might reframe this to, *"Yes, of course I've made mistakes before, but I've also learned from them and succeeded in many areas."*

Positive Affirmations: Create a list of positive affirmations that counter your self-doubt and reinforce your strengths. Repeat these affirmations daily, especially during moments of doubt. Phrases like *"I am capable," "I learn from my experiences,"* and *"I am worthy of success"* can help build a more empowering mindset over time.

***Visualization*:** Use your imagination to see yourself successfully overcoming a situation that would ordinarily trigger self-doubt. Imagine how you would feel, your actions, and the positive outcomes. Create a mental blueprint for success, making it easier to react confidently in real-life situations.

Building Confidence Through Action

Taking action is also important to breaking the cycle of self-doubt. Confidence and self-efficacy[1] are built through experience—by facing challenges and proving to yourself that you are capable. Even small steps can make a significant difference in shifting your mindset from one of doubt to one of belief in your abilities.

You can build confidence and self-belief by taking proactive steps to challenge self-doubt. Each action, no matter how small, is a step toward breaking free from the cycle of self-doubt and moving closer to a more empowered, fulfilling life.

---

1. According to the American Psychological Association, "Self-efficacy refers to an individual's belief in his or her capacity to execute behaviors necessary to produce specific performance attainments . . . [It] reflects confidence in the ability to exert control over one's own motivation, behavior, and social environment."

From Self-Doubt to Self-Belief

Overcoming self-doubt and building self-belief starts by recognizing that self-doubt is a learned behavior. It can be unlearned and replaced with a more empowering mindset. You have already begun this journey by exploring self-doubt, understanding its triggers, and identifying how it manifests in your life. Each additional step you take toward self-awareness and self-reflection helps to transform your inner dialogue from one of doubt to one of confidence.

This path toward self-belief requires patience, practice, and perseverance. It involves challenging negative thoughts, embracing vulnerability, and taking bold, courageous action, even when you don't feel ready. But every effort you make to confront your fears and step out of your comfort zone builds resilience and reinforces your belief in your capabilities. Remember, self-belief is not about being perfect or never experiencing doubt. It's about trusting yourself enough to move forward despite any doubts that may arise.

Everyone is capable of transformation. No matter how entrenched self-doubt may seem, you can change your internal narrative and start building a solid foundation of self-belief. By committing to this journey and taking small but consistent steps, you can shift your mindset and unlock your full potential.

It's time to embrace the possibility of change and prepare to awaken your Inner Warrior.

Prepare to Meet Your Inner Warrior

As we move forward, it's time to introduce your Inner Warrior—a powerful force within you that can serve as a counterbalance to self-doubt. Your Inner Warrior embodies qualities such as courage, resilience, and self-belief. It represents the part of you that is brave enough to face challenges head-on, strong enough to bounce back from setbacks, and confident enough to believe in your worth and capabilities.

Your Inner Warrior is not fearless or invincible; it just recognizes that fear and doubt are natural parts of life but they don't control your actions or define your worth. Your Inner Warrior pushes through your fears, takes risks, and pursues goals with absolute determination and confidence. It encourages you to trust yourself and your abilities, even when the path ahead is unclear.

In the next chapter, we will discuss awakening the Inner Warrior and learn how to harness its strength to overcome self-doubt and build a more empowered, fulfilling life. You will learn practical ways to build courage, resilience, and self-belief, helping you move forward with greater confidence and purpose.

Chapter 4
Awakening Your Inner Warrior

"Do not speak badly of yourself, for the warrior that is inside you hears your words and is lessened by them"
David Gemmell

Deep within each of us lies a powerful ally—our Inner Warrior. This part of ourselves represents courage, resilience, and an unwavering confidence in our abilities. While self-doubt diminishes our confidence and holds us back, our Inner Warrior propels us forward, helping us face challenges head-on and pursue our goals with determination and strength. Awakening your Inner Warrior means tapping into this source of inner strength and learning to harness it to overcome obstacles, build confidence, and live a more fulfilled life.

In this chapter, you will meet your Inner Warrior and learn to cultivate the qualities that define this empowering presence. We will discuss strategies for building resilience, courage, and strengthening self-belief, all essential components of the Inner Warrior mindset. Connecting with your Inner Warrior helps you to quiet the voice of self-doubt, take bold actions, and overcome life's challenges with confidence and grace.

Meet Your Inner Warrior

Your Inner Warrior is a powerful internal presence that embodies courage, resilience, and self-belief. It represents the part of you that stands firm in the face of adversity, overcomes obstacles, and faces challenges with unwavering determination and confidence. Unlike your Inner Critic, which tends to undermine your confidence and fuel self-doubt, your Inner Warrior is your champion, encouraging you to push beyond any perceived limits and achieve your true potential.

The Inner Warrior is a vital counterbalance to the Inner Critic. While the Inner Critic may whisper: *"You're just not good enough,"* the Inner Warrior says: *"You have the strength, courage, and resilience to overcome any obstacles."* It reminds you of your worth, reinforces your confidence, and motivates you to take action despite any lingering fear or uncertainty. By awakening and nurturing your Inner Warrior, you can learn to quiet the negative voice of the Inner Critic and replace self-doubt with self-belief.

The 6 Main Traits of the Inner Warrior

The first and most prominent trait of the Inner Warrior is ***courage***, driving you to confront your fears and take action despite uncertainty and the risk of complete failure. Courage does not man being fearless; instead, it means acknowledging your fears and choosing to move forward anyway. It means facing the unknown, stepping outside your comfort zone, and focusing on opportunity, not risk. The Inner Warrior draws on courage to overcome the paralyzing effects of fear, encouraging you to take bold steps toward your goals and dreams.

Bravery, the second trait, is closely related to courage and is another key trait of your Inner Warrior. Bravery involves standing firm in the face of adversity, making difficult decisions, and pursuing what is right, especially when those decisions are challenged and/or criticized by others. Your Inner Warrior understands that fear is a natural part of the human experience but does not allow it to dictate actions or limit potential.

The third defining trait of your Inner Warrior is ***resilience***—the ability to bounce back from setbacks, adapt to challenges, and keep moving forward despite adversity. Resilient people maintain a positive outlook, even when things don't go as planned. The Inner Warrior recovers quickly from difficulties and views obstacles as opportunities for growth and learning. Resilience helps you to endure life's ups and downs with grace, remaining steadfast in the pursuit of your long-term goals.

Perseverance, the fourth trait, is another facet of resilience, requiring effort and commitment, even when progress is slow or obstacles arise. The Inner Warrior shows an unwavering determination to keep going, no matter how tough the journey becomes. Perseverance means staying focused on your most important objectives and pushing through challenges, setbacks, and doubts. It's the Inner Warrior's resolve that keeps you to committed to your path to emerge stronger on the other side.

Confidence, the fifth trait, is another characteristic of the Inner Warrior.

Now, I want to briefly pause here.

Confidence is grossly misunderstood in society today. People who come across to others as brash, sassy, loud, and overly argumentative commonly label themselves as *'confident.'* In reality, these traits are really a (not so subtle) mask used to hide ignorance, insecurities, and deep-seated fears.

Real confidence doesn't try to be *'right'* all of the time, tell people off, and certainly isn't the loudest voice in the room. It is a *quiet strength*, a sense of assurance in your abilities and judgment, a belief that you can handle whatever comes your way.

Confidence is also not arrogant or overestimating your capabilities; instead, it is a realistic understanding of your strengths and trusting yourself to make decisions and take decisive action when needed. The Inner Warrior naturally exudes confidence by reminding you of your achievements, skills, and experiences, helping you face new challenges with a sense of assurance.

Closely connected to confidence is *self-belief*, the sixth trait, which is a deep-rooted faith in your ability to succeed despite life's inevitable challenges. Self-belief is the conviction that you have the inner fortitude, resilience, and courage to achieve your goals, regardless of external circumstances. It is unwavering trust in your potential and self-worth, reinforcing the idea that you are capable of overcoming obstacles and thriving.

Together, these six characteristics—courage, bravery, resilience, perseverance, confidence and self-belief—define the Inner Warrior. By cultivating these traits, you strengthen your Inner Warrior, helping you face challenges with courage, bounce back from setbacks with resilience, and move forward with confidence.

Recognizing Strengths and Overcoming Resistance

The first step in discovering your Inner Warrior is recognizing your unique strengths, talents, and qualities. Everyone has unique talents, abilities and attributes that mirror their Inner Warrior's courage, resilience, and self-belief. Start by taking some time to reflect on your past experiences. Think about times when you faced challenges head-on, overcame obstacles, or pushed through difficult circumstances. Think about times when you demonstrated courage by taking risks, speaking up for yourself or others, or by stepping out of your comfort zone.

Reflect on situations where you showed resilience by recovering from setbacks or adapting to a new, challenging circumstance. These moments reveal your Inner Warrior, showcasing your ability to persevere despite adversity. Recall times when you trusted in your abilities, made confident decisions, or pursued a goal with determination. These experiences are a testament to your inner strength and potential.

By identifying these strengths and qualities, you start to connect with your Inner Warrior. Acknowledge and celebrate these traits, understanding that they are a fundamental part of who you are. Recognizing your strengths is crucial in awakening your Inner Warrior, helping you build a solid foundation of confidence and strength.

As you awaken your Inner Warrior, you will undoubtedly encounter resistance. This commonly takes the form of doubt, fear, or feelings of unworthiness, arising from deeply ingrained patterns of self-doubt and negative self-talk from your Inner Critic. You might find yourself questioning whether you really have what it takes to succeed or fearing that you will fail miserably if you try. This internal resistance can be a significant barrier to growth, preventing you from fully embracing your potential.

To overcome this resistance, it is important to recognize it for what it is—an emotional response triggered by change and uncertainty, not a measure of your true capabilities. Begin with self-compassion, understanding that feeling uncertain or hesitant when facing something new is completely normal. Instead of judging yourself harshly for having these feelings, approach them with kindness and empathy. Know that everyone experiences doubt and fear at times, and that these emotions do not define your worth or potential.

Visualization and Positive Self-Talk

Visualization is another powerful tool for awakening your Inner Warrior. By picturing yourself as strong, capable, and courageous, you reinforce the qualities of your Inner Warrior and embody them in daily life. Visualization helps you mentally rehearse facing challenges with confidence, which, in turn, builds the strength needed to act with courage in real-life situations.

Here's a visualization exercise to try:

1. ***Find a Quiet Space:*** Find a quiet, comfortable place where you won't be disturbed. Sit or lie down in a relaxed position and close your eyes.

2. ***Focus on Your Breathing:*** Take a few deep breaths, in-

haling slowly through your nose and exhaling through your mouth. With each breath, allow your body to relax, letting go of any tension or stress.

3. ***Create a Mental Image***: Imagine yourself in a situation where you need your Inner Warrior. You may be facing a difficult challenge, making a bold decision, or standing up for yourself. Visualize yourself as strong, confident, and courageous in this situation.

4. ***Engage Your Senses***: As you visualize, engage all your senses. What do you see, hear, and feel in this scenario? Imagine the confidence in your stance, the steadiness in your voice, and the clarity in your mind as you take action. Picture successfully overcoming the challenge with strength and determination.

5. ***Affirm Your Strength***: As you continue to visualize, repeat affirmations that reinforce your inner strength. Phrases like *"I am strong and capable," "I face challenges with courage,"* and *"My Inner Warrior supports me"* can help solidify this powerful image in your mind.

6. ***Return to the Present***: When you're ready, slowly bring your awareness back to the present moment. Take a few deep breaths, gently open your eyes, and carry the feeling of strength and confidence throughout the day.

This visualization exercise can help you connect more deeply with your Inner Warrior, building mental and emotional resilience each day.

Affirmations and positive self-talk are also essential tools for silencing your Inner Critic. By focusing on empowering thoughts and beliefs, you cultivate a mindset full of courage, resilience, and self-belief.

Affirmations are short, positive statements that you repeat to yourself regularly. They help to reprogram your mind, replacing negative or self-doubting thoughts with empowering ones.

Here are some examples of affirmations focused on strengthening your Inner Warrior:

- *"I am courageous and face challenges with strength."*
- *"I trust in my abilities and make confident decisions."*
- *"I am resilient and capable of overcoming any obstacle."*
- *"My Inner Warrior guides me to success and fulfillment."*
- *"I believe in myself and my power to achieve great things."*

To use affirmations, choose a few that resonate with your values and purpose and repeat them daily. You can say them aloud, write them down, or even create visual reminders to place around your home or workspace. The key is consistency—regular repetition helps reinforce and integrate these positive beliefs into your mind.

Positive self-talk complements affirmations by encouraging you to speak to yourself in a supportive and empowering way. When you catch yourself thinking in a negative way, consciously replace them with positive, affirming language. For example, if you find yourself thinking, *"I can't do this,"* counter it with, *"I am capable and strong, and I can handle this."* Over time, this practice shifts your inner dialogue from one of doubt to one of self-belief.

Build a Relationship with Your Inner Warrior

Like any relationship, it is important to build and cultivate a relationship with your Inner Warrior. This begins with listening to its voice. Your Inner Warrior is always there, ready to offer guidance and support, especially in times of doubt or fear. But, more often than not, its voice is drowned out by the Inner Critic's louder, more critical overtones.

Start by setting aside quiet moments in your day to connect with your Inner Warrior. This can be done through meditation, mindfulness, or simply taking a few minutes to sit in silence.

Journaling is an excellent tool for facilitating this inner dialogue. To kickstart the process, consider these questions:

- *"What strengths does my Inner Warrior see that I may not recognize?"*

- *"How can I draw on my Inner Warrior's courage to face this challenge?"*

- *"What wisdom does my Inner Warrior have for me today?"*

- *"When have I shown resilience, and how can I continue to build on that?"*

- *"What steps can I take to display the qualities of my Inner Warrior?"*

As you journal, allow your thoughts to flow freely, and don't worry about grammar or structure. The goal is to connect with your Inner Warrior and hear its voice. Over time, this practice can help you build a stronger relationship with this powerful part of yourself, making it easier to tap into its guidance and strength when you need it most.

Trusting Your Inner Warrior

Trust is another essential component of any relationship, including your Inner Warrior. To fully benefit from its strength and guidance, you need to trust its wisdom and trust in your ability to embody its qualities. This allows you to rely on your Inner Warrior when faced with fear or uncertainty.

Building trust with your Inner Warrior takes time and practice. Start by taking small, courageous actions that align with your Inner Warrior's voice. These actions don't have to be monumental; they can be as simple as speaking up in a meeting, setting a boundary in a relationship, or trying something new that scares you. The key is to take actions that push you slightly out of your comfort zone and to show willingness to trust your inner strength.

After taking a small action that pushes you outside of your comfort zone, take some time to reflect on how the experience turned out.

Ask yourself:

- *"How did it feel to take this action? What emotions did I experience?"*

- *"What did I learn about myself and my capabilities?"*

- *"How did my Inner Warrior support me in this moment?"*

- *"What can I do to continue building trust with my Inner Warrior?"*

Reflecting on questions like these helps to reinforce the connection with your Inner Warrior and builds confidence in its guidance. The more you work on trusting your Inner Warrior, the stronger its voice will become, helping you face challenges with greater confidence.

Your Inner Warrior in Action: Facing Tough Decisions and Challenges

Your Inner Warrior supports strategic decision-making by encouraging bold choices that align with your long-term values and goals. When facing difficult decisions, it's easy to be apprehensive, leading you to the safer, more comfortable path. However, listening to the voice of your Inner Warrior will cause you to carefully consider what really matters to you, pushing you to take risks that align with your authentic self.

To illustrate, imagine you are considering a career change that excites you, but also comes with uncertainty and risk. Your Inner Critic will constantly warn you about the potential for failure or the security you'd give up. But your Inner Warrior encourages you to trust your abilities and follow your passion, knowing that this choice aligns with your long-term values and will bring you closer to your financial or career goals. By tapping into the strength of your Inner Warrior, you can make tough decisions with courage and conviction.

Another scenario might involve the need to set boundaries in a relationship. Maybe you've been avoiding a difficult conversation with a close friend or family member because you fear conflict or rejection. Your Inner Warrior, though, recognizes the importance of maintaining healthy boundaries and supportive relationships. Listening to its voice gives you the courage to speak your truth and establish boundaries that respect your needs.

Remember that challenges and setbacks are inevitable in life, but how you respond to them makes all the difference. Your Inner Warrior equips you with a resilient mindset, allowing you to overcome obstacles with grace and determination. Rather than viewing setbacks as failures or signs of inadequacy, the Inner Warrior sees them as opportunities for growth and learning.

Even when facing a professional setback or a personal loss, your Inner Warrior keeps moving forward when the path is uncertain. It reminds you that resilience is more about getting back up than never falling down. By focusing on your strengths instead of your vulnerabilities, your Inner Warrior helps you maintain a positive outlook and stay committed to your goals.

Sustaining Your Inner Warrior

To keep your Inner Warrior strong and resilient, you must include daily habits that nurture its qualities. These practices reinforce courage, resilience, and self-belief, allowing you to maintain a connection with your Inner Warrior, especially during difficult times.

Gratitude Journaling: Taking a few moments each day to reflect on what you are grateful for can significantly enhance your mindset. By focusing on what's positive in your life, you develop a greater sense of appreciation and contentment, which counteracts the harmful effects of self-doubt. Start each day by writing down three things you are grateful for. These can be simple things, like a kind gesture from a friend, or a moment of peace in your day. This helps shift your focus from what's lacking to what's abundant in your life, reinforcing a positive, warrior-like mindset.

Physical Exercise: Regular physical activity is another powerful way to strengthen your Inner Warrior. Exercise improves physical health as well as mental and emotional well-being. Running, yoga, or strength training can help build resilience by challenging your body and mind to push through discomfort and overcome obstacles. Exercise also releases endorphins, boosting your mood and increasing confidence.

Consistency is key in these practices. Just as warriors train regularly to maintain their strength and skills, you must commit to these daily routines to sustain your Inner Warrior's strength. By incorporating gratitude journaling, physical exercise, and meditation into your routine, you create a foundation for ongoing growth and resilience, helping your Inner Warrior to thrive.

As you continue to sustain your Inner Warrior, it is essential to practice self-compassion and patience. Growth and transformation are not linear processes; they involve setbacks, challenges, and moments of doubt. It is natural to have days when you feel disconnected from your Inner Warrior or struggle to maintain a positive attitude. During these times, be gentle with yourself and recognize that this is a normal part of the journey.

Self-compassion means that you treat yourself with the same kindness, empathy, and understanding that you would give a close friend. When facing difficulties or mistakes, rather than criticizing yourself, acknowledge your feelings and offer yourself words of encouragement and support. Remember that these moments do not define your worth or potential.

Patience is also an essential quality to cultivate on this journey. Building a strong relationship with your Inner Warrior takes time and effort. There will be ups and downs, but each step you take, no matter how small, contributes to your overall growth and development. Trust in the process and permit yourself to move at your own pace. Every moment is an opportunity to learn and grow; awakening your Inner Warrior is an ongoing process.

The Connection Between Self-Belief and Your Inner Warrior

Your Inner Warrior helps you to develop self-belief. When you tap into its qualities, you learn to face challenges head-on, persevere through setbacks, and make decisions that are aligned with your true values. These experiences promote self-reliance and self-assurance, which are essential components of self-belief.

Courage nudges you to step outside your comfort zone and take risks, showing that you can overcome fear and manage uncertainty. Confidence grows each time you rely on your Inner Warrior to make bold decisions and take decisive action, proving to yourself that you have the strength and wisdom to thrive in the face of life's challenges and complexities. Together, these qualities lay the groundwork for cultivating a strong sense of self-belief, helping you move forward with complete faith in your potential.

In the next chapter, we will examine self-belief in more detail, including how it influences our thoughts and actions and why it is vital for achieving personal fulfillment. You will learn how to identify and challenge limiting beliefs that undermine your confidence and replace them with supportive thoughts.

Chapter 5
Overcoming Limiting Beliefs

"Life has no limitations, except the ones you make."
Les Brown

Self-belief is the foundation of confidence and success. It's the unwavering trust in your abilities and judgment that supports decisive action and pursuit of your goals. While the Inner Warrior provides strength and courage, true self-belief fuels the confidence to move forward with determination.

In this chapter, we'll focus on building self-belief by understanding its importance and identifying the limiting beliefs that often hold you back. You'll learn to challenge these negative thoughts and strengthen your confidence moving forward.

What is Self-Belief?

Self-belief is confidence in your abilities, judgment, and potential to succeed. It is the trust you place in yourself to handle challenges, make decisions, and pursue goals with determination.

It's important to distinguish self-confidence from arrogance and overconfidence. Arrogance and overconfidence stem from inflated perceptions and are not grounded in reality. In contrast, self-belief is based on a realistic view of your strengths and abilities. It builds on self-awareness, where you acknowledge both your potential and limitations, helping you to act confidently but humbly.

Self-belief is essential for personal growth and resilience. It is the driving force that enables you to take risks, embrace challenges, and recover from setbacks. Without self-belief, it is easy to be overwhelmed by self-doubt and then fear, making it difficult to reach your goals. Self-belief is not something you are born with; it is developed and strengthened over time.

The Foundations of Self-Belief

Self-awareness is a fundamental building block of self-belief. It means understanding yourself—your strengths, weaknesses, and areas for growth. Thus, providing a holistic view of who you are and what you are capable of achieving. By knowing yourself, you can make more informed decisions, set realistic goals, and recognize your progress over time, all of which contribute to a stronger sense of self-belief.

Another aspect of self-belief is *self-acceptance*, which is the practice of taking yourself at face value, including your weaknesses and mistakes. It recognizes that being human means having flaws and making errors, and that these do not diminish your worth. Accepting who you are creates a realistic and compassionate view of yourself, which is essential for self-belief.

When you practice self-acceptance, you free yourself from the pressure of needing to be perfect. Instead, you can focus solely on your overall growth and development, knowing that it is okay to have setbacks and challenges along the way. This level of acceptance also helps to build self-belief, as it allows you to trust yourself despite your imperfections.

Self-love and ***self-compassion*** are additional methods for strengthening self-belief. Self-love involves treating yourself with kindness and care, while self-compassion means being understanding and forgiving toward yourself, especially when you make mistakes or face difficulties. Both of these practices encourage a positive and supportive relationship with yourself, which further enhances self-belief.

I want to pause for just a moment and emphasize that many times we feel lost in life. We simply don't know how to love ourselves. Interestingly, we are taught from an early age how to love and care for others, but somehow the importance of treating ourselves with the same level of kindness is never conveyed.

Here are some practices that you may find helpful:

Self-Care Routines: Engage in regular self-care activities that nourish your body, mind, and spirit. This might include exercise, healthy eating, spending time with close friends and loved ones, or hobbies that bring you happiness and satisfaction. Taking care of yourself is a powerful way to reinforce self-love and show yourself that you matter.

Self-Forgiveness: Practice forgiving yourself for past mistakes and letting go of guilt or regret. Understand that everyone makes mistakes and that these moments are opportunities for learning and growth. By forgiving yourself, you create space for self-compassion and move forward with greater confidence.

By building a foundation of self-awareness, self-acceptance, and self-love, you can cultivate a deep and long-lasting sense of self-belief. These practices help you recognize your worth, embrace your strengths and weaknesses, and treat yourself with kindness and respect, all of which are essential for a purposeful, fulfilling life.

Identify and Reframe Limiting Beliefs

Limiting beliefs are negative beliefs that hinder your motivation and success. They are internal thoughts that make you feel incapable, undeserving, or unworthy of your goals. These beliefs often arise from past experiences and societal influences, significantly undermining your self-belief and decision-making.

Some common limiting beliefs include:

- *"I'm not good enough."*

- *"I don't deserve success."*

- *"I'm too old/young to start something new."*

- *"I'll never be able to change."*

- *"People like me don't succeed."*

- *"I'm not smart/talented enough."*

To overcome these limiting beliefs, start by identifying the specific ideas that hold you back. Reflect on situations where you felt hesitant or unsure of yourself and think about what beliefs were triggering those feelings. Write down any recurring negative thoughts that come to mind, and be honest with yourself about how these beliefs have influenced your actions and decisions.

Once you have identified your limiting beliefs, the next step is to challenge and reframe them. Start by questioning the validity of each belief.

Ask yourself:

- *Is this belief based on facts or assumptions?*

- *What evidence do I have that contradicts this belief?*

- *Have I succeeded in similar situations in the past?*

- *Would I say this to a friend in the same situation?*

By critically examining these beliefs, you will begin to see that many of them are not grounded in reality, but are instead based on fear, insecurity, or past experiences.

After challenging your limiting beliefs, work on reframing them into more positive statements.

For instance:

- *"I'm not good enough"* turns into *"I am capable of learning and growing."*

- *"I don't deserve success"* turns into *"I am worthy of success and happiness."*

- *"I'll never be able to change"* turns into *"I have the power to change and improve."*

Reframing your beliefs helps to create a more supportive internal dialogue and reinforces a positive self-image. Practice repeating these new, empowering statements regularly to replace the old limiting beliefs with a more constructive mindset.

Rewriting Your Story

With the exception of marketers, advertisers, politicians, and the news media, very few people realize just how powerful stories and storytelling can be. A skillful attorney can make a ruthless murderer seem human—even likable in some cases simply by telling the right story.

Likewise, the stories we tell ourselves shape our self-belief and influence our actions. If you have been feeding yourself a narrative filled with doubt, fear, and limitation, it's time to rewrite it. Changing your internal story leads to greater confidence and self-assurance, helping you to break free from the limits of your past experiences.

Reflect on positive experiences to create a new narrative that inspires you. Write it down and revisit it often, especially when you feel self-doubt creeping in. Remember, you have the power to shape your story and define your future. By rewriting your internal story in a way that highlights your strengths and potential, you cultivate self-belief and gain a stronger sense of identity.

Alright. Let's pause for a moment.

Now, I'm not gonna get all *'woo-woo'* on you here, but let's take another look at affirmations and self-talk.

Remember, what you say affects how you think; and vice-versa.

So, one of the most powerful ways to rewrite the story you tell yourself is to use affirmations. As we've discussed previously, affirmations are the positive statements that you repeat to yourself to challenge and overcome self-sabotaging thoughts and negative beliefs.

Affirmations are so powerful in rewriting your internal dialogue because they can effectively rewire the brain for positive thinking. By consistently repeating affirmations, you eventually create new neural pathways that promote a more optimistic outlook and positive self-perceptions.

Research in neuroscience indicates that our brains can change and adapt in response to new experiences and repeated behaviors, a concept known as **neuroplasticity**. When you use affirmations regularly, you effectively train your brain to focus on positive thoughts and beliefs, replacing negative patterns implanted by your Inner Critic that contribute to self-doubt. Over time, this practice will help you develop a stronger sense of self-belief and confidence in your abilities.

Your affirmations are unique—guided by your long-term goals and values. Thus, when creating affirmations, make them personal, positive, and aligned with your true self.

When choosing which affirmations to create, consider these guidelines:

Be Specific: Choose affirmations that address specific areas of self-belief you want to improve. Instead of vague statements like *"I am good,"* opt for more targeted affirmations instead such as *"I am capable of achieving my goals."*

Use Present Tense: Frame your affirmations in the present tense as if they are already true. This approach helps your brain internalize the statement as a current reality rather than a future possibility. For example, say, *"I am confident in my abilities,"* rather than *"I will be confident in my abilities."*

Keep It Positive: Focus on what you want to achieve, not what you want to avoid. Avoid negative words like *"don't"* or *"can't."* Instead, use positive language that emphasizes your strengths and potential.

Make It Believable: Create affirmations that resonate with you and feel authentic. While it's important to challenge your limiting beliefs, your affirmations should be within the realm of possibility for your mind to truly believe them.

Positive self-talk is another important tool for counteracting the Inner Critic. Now, while I'm not suggesting walking downtown in broad daylight openly talking to yourself, changing your internal mental dialogue can prove helpful in counteracting limiting beliefs. The process involves consciously choosing to speak to yourself in a supportive and encouraging tone, focusing on your strengths and abilities rather than allowing your Inner Critic to dominate your thoughts with perceived flaws or failures.

Build Confidence by Taking Action

If you've ever heard the saying, *"Talk the talk and walk the walk,"* you understand that confidence is built not just through positive thinking but through action. Taking action, even in small steps, is a powerful way to build confidence and self-belief. When you stop ruminating and take action, you prove to yourself that you are capable of moving forward in life despite fear or uncertainty. Each step you take, no matter how minor, is evidence that you can handle challenges and achieve your goals.

This concept is sometimes referred to as *"confidence through competence."* As you develop your skills and abilities through practice and experimentation, you naturally become more confident in your capabilities. Competence breeds confidence, as each success reinforces your belief in yourself and your potential. By consistently taking action and building on your skills, you create a solid foundation of self-assurance that motivates you to take on even greater challenges.

Setting realistic and achievable goals is also vital for building confidence through action. Goals provide specific direction and motivation, giving you a sense of purpose and a clear roadmap for progress. To set useful goals, it's important to make sure they align with your values, not those of others.

To avoid feeling stressed out at the thought of goal setting, break down larger goals into smaller, manageable steps. This approach makes the journey less overwhelming and allows you to celebrate small victories along the way, which builds further momentum and confidence.

Celebrate Success. Learn from Failure.

Celebrating your success, no matter how small, is crucial to building confidence and reinforcing self-belief. Recalling your achievements validates your efforts and provides positive reinforcement, encouraging you to keep moving forward each day. Take time to reflect on what you've accomplished, reward yourself in some meaningful way for your hard work, and allow yourself to feel proud of your progress. These celebrations are important reminders that you are capable and worthy of success.

Equally important is learning from failures. We all make mistakes, but how we respond to them makes all the difference. View failures as opportunities for growth and learning. Ask yourself what you can learn from the experience, what you might do differently next time, and how this knowledge can help you improve. By accepting failures with a growth mindset, you turn challenges into valuable lessons that strengthen your resilience and self-belief.

Incorporating these practices into your life—taking action, setting achievable goals, celebrating successes, and learning from failures—will all help you develop confidence and build a stronger foundation of self-belief. With each step you take, you reinforce your ability to grow and succeed.

Anticipate and Manage Setbacks

Setbacks and challenges are inevitable, but they can test even the strongest self-belief. It is important to be prepared to manage them effectively. Recognizing that setbacks are normal allows you to approach them with a proactive mindset, using them as opportunities to grow rather than letting them erode your self-confidence.

When a setback occurs, take enough time to process the situation. Ask yourself what you can learn from the experience, what you might do differently next time, and how you can use this knowledge to improve.

Also, don't be afraid to reach out for support when needed. Whether it's talking to a trusted friend, mentor, or mental health professional, seeking support can provide valuable perspective and encouragement during challenging times. Sharing your experiences with others can help you feel less isolated and remind you that setbacks are a normal part of the journey.

During difficult times, it's important to remember that self-belief is not about being perfect or never experiencing doubt; it's about being persistent and staying committed to your growth and goals, even when things get tough.

In the next chapter, we'll look at some strategies for balancing your Inner Critic and Inner Warrior. You will learn how to manage the voices of doubt and fear while nurturing the courage, resilience, and self-assurance of your Inner Warrior.

Chapter 6
Balancing Your Inner Critic and Inner Warrior

"Balance is not something you find, it's something you create"

Jana Kingsford

Up until now, we've given our Inner Critic a pretty bad rap, highlighting its tendency to be overly harsh and counterproductive. But it can also serve as the voice of caution, keeping us from making errors by being too hasty or taking on too much at one time. On the other hand, the Inner Warrior embodies courage and self-belief, encouraging you to pursue your goals aggressively and confidently.

In this chapter, we will look at finding a healthy balance between these two internal voices. By managing your Inner Critic, you can reduce its negative impact, turning criticism into motivation for improvement. At the same time, nurturing your Inner Warrior builds a stronger foundation of self-belief. Working together, this dichotomy of opposing voices helps create a harmonious inner dialogue.

Achieving Inner Balance

Balancing the Inner Critic and the Inner Warrior involves using both of these internal voices to your advantage, rather than allowing only one to completely dominate your thoughts and actions. The Inner Critic often points out areas for improvement, prompting self-reflection and growth. But if left unchecked, it can become overly critical and undermine your confidence. On the other hand, the Inner Warrior provides strength and courage, encouraging you to take risks and believe in yourself.

The goal of balancing these voices is not to eliminate your Inner Critic, but to manage it successfully, making sure it serves a constructive purpose. By differentiating between when your Inner Critic is offering valuable insights and when it is being excessively harsh, you can respond in a way that promotes growth. This inner balance allows both voices to manage your decision-making process and personal development.

When these two voices work in harmony with each other, you make decisions with greater thoughtfulness and confidence, rooted in greater self-awareness. This harmony boosts emotional resilience, helping you tackle setbacks and challenges without succumbing to self-doubt or complacency. Moreover, a balanced internal dialogue leads to a more harmonious and productive mindset. Instead of being paralyzed by criticism or recklessly overconfident, you can assess situations objectively and take action with both courage and caution.

Recognize When Your Inner Critic is Taking Over

An overactive Inner Critic can significantly impact your mental and emotional well-being, so it's important to recognize when this voice is dominating your thoughts and actions.

Here are some signs that your Inner Critic may be taking over:

Constant Self-Criticism: You frequently engage in negative self-talk, focusing on your perceived flaws and mistakes. This might include harsh, irrational judgments about your abilities, appearance, or worth.

Perfectionism: You set unrealistically high standards for yourself and feel like nothing you do is ever good enough. This chronic perfectionism can lead to feelings of inadequacy and dissatisfaction, regardless of your achievements.

Procrastination: You delay or avoid tasks because you fear making mistakes or not meeting up to expectations. Procrastination most commonly stems from a deep-seated fear of failure or judgment, driven, in part, by an overly critical inner voice.

Avoidance of New Challenges: You avoid trying new things or stepping out of your comfort zone because you fear failure or criticism. The Inner Critic convinces you that you are not capable or ready, preventing you from taking risks and growing.

Reflect on recent experiences of self-doubt or negativity. Identify situations where your Inner Critic influenced your thoughts and actions, and consider how this affected your decisions. Acknowledging these patterns is essential for managing your Inner Critic.

To better understand your own personal triggers, think about past situations where your Inner Critic was particularly active. Identify common themes or patterns that emerge, and consider how these triggers influenced your thoughts and behaviors. By becoming more aware of your triggers, you can prepare yourself to respond appropriately when your Inner Critic is vocal, maintaining a balanced mindset.

Managing Your Inner Critic

Cognitive restructuring is a powerful technique for identifying, challenging, and changing negative thought patterns associated with the Inner Critic. This method helps you become aware of irrational or unhelpful thoughts, examine their validity, and replace them with more balanced and constructive thoughts.

Here are some ways to accomplish this:

Recognize Irrational Thoughts: Start by paying attention to your inner dialogue, especially in moments of self-doubt or when you are criticized by others. Notice when your Inner Critic is speaking and identify the specific thoughts it is using. These might be statements like, *"I always mess things up"* or *"I'm not good enough."*

Carefully Weigh the Evidence: Once you've identified a negative thought, consider the evidence for and against it. Ask yourself questions like, *"What evidence do I have that supports this thought?"* and *"What evidence contradicts it?"* Often, you'll find that these negative thoughts are exaggerated or based on past experiences that don't reflect your current reality.

Replace with Balanced Thoughts: After evaluating the evidence, replace the irrational thought with a more balanced and constructive one. For example, instead of, *"I always mess things up,"* you might replace it with, *"I've made mistakes before, but I've also learned from them and improved."* This new thought should be realistic, positive, and supportive.

Practice Regularly: Cognitive restructuring is most effective when practiced regularly. Make it a habit to challenge your Inner Critic whenever it arises, gradually retraining your mind to think in a more positive and balanced way.

Setting healthy but firm boundaries with your Inner Critic is another important step to prevent it from dominating your thoughts and emotions. By creating distance between yourself and your Inner Critic, you can acknowledge its presence without allowing it to dictate your actions.

Here's how:

Limit Engagement: Set a time limit for how long you will engage with critical thoughts. For instance, you could decide to spend no more than five minutes acknowledging and reflecting on these negative thoughts before moving on to something more constructive.

Box it Up: Visualize putting the Inner Critic in a mental *"box"* or creating some other type of barrier between you and it. Imagine yourself stepping back from your Inner Critic, watching from a distance without engaging with its negativity.

Practice Self-Assertion: When your Inner Critic becomes more vocal, assert your intention to not let it control you. Acknowledge its presence, but remind yourself that you are in charge of your thoughts and actions. You might say something like, *"I hear you, but I choose not to let this affect me right now."*

Strengthening Your Inner Warrior

Reinforcing positive self-belief is essential for strengthening your Inner Warrior while managing the influence of your Inner Critic. When you choose to focus on your strengths, accomplishments, and future potential, you allow your Inner Warrior to guide you through challenges with confidence and resilience. A mindset rooted in self-belief helps you trust in your abilities and remain motivated, even in the face of adversity.

Begin your day with positive affirmations that remind you of your worth and capabilities. Choose statements that resonate with you, such as *"I am capable of overcoming any challenge I encounter today"* or *"I trust in my ability to succeed."* Repeat these affirmations regularly to reinforce a positive attitude and healthy self-image.

As you journal, build a list of past successes and the strengths that contributed to those achievements. Review this list regularly, especially when you're feeling doubtful or discouraged. Reminding yourself of what you've already accomplished will boost your confidence and strengthen your Inner Warrior's voice.

Emotional resilience is another key factor in keeping your Inner Warrior strong. Resilience helps you bounce back from challenges with greater ease, maintaining a positive outlook and a strong sense of self-confidence. Doing this trains your Inner Warrior to handle life's difficulties without being overwhelmed by negativity or self-doubt.

Regularly focusing on what you're grateful for shifts your perspective from what's missing to what's abundant in your life. This encourages a positive mindset, making it easier to stay resilient in the face of adversity. Additionally, surround yourself with supportive individuals who encourage your growth and uplift your spirit. Whether it's friends, family, or mentors, having a strong support network can provide reassurance and motivation needed to stay resilient during tough times.

Making Your Inner Critic and Inner Warrior Work Together Harmoniously

While our Inner Critic can sometimes manifest as a harsh and judgmental voice, it can be changed into a powerful force that contributes to our personal growth and development. By converting negative criticism into constructive feedback, your Inner Critic can help you identify areas for improvement and motivate you to strive for your best.

Consider the following approach:

Identify the Core Concern: When you notice your Inner Critic being harsh, take a moment to pause and ask yourself what the core concern or underlying message might be. For example, if your Inner Critic says, *"You always mess things up,"* the core concern could be an underlying fear of failure or a strong desire to succeed.

Reframe the Message: Once you've identified the core concern, reframe the Inner Critic's message into constructive feedback. Instead of *"You always mess things up,"* reframe it as, *"I want to do my best, and there are some steps I can take to improve next time."* This approach turns a negative statement into a constructive one, focused on growth and improvement.

Focus on Specific Actions: Encourage your Inner Critic to be specific about what could be improved. For example, rather than saying, *"You're not good enough,"* your Inner Critic could say, *"Next time, I could prepare more thoroughly to feel more confident."* This approach to reframing shifts the focus from a blanket judgment to actionable feedback.

By working to transform your Inner Critic into a constructive, action-oriented voice, you can harness its insights for self-improvement without allowing it to undermine your confidence and self-belief.

Creating an Open Dialogue

Creating an open dialogue between your Inner Critic and Inner Warrior allows both voices to be heard and balanced. This creates a more nuanced internal conversation where the Inner Critic provides constructive feedback, and the Inner Warrior offers encouragement and support. By integrating these two voices, you can achieve a healthier and more balanced, harmonious mindset.

One popular exercise is to write fictitious letters. For instance, write a letter from your Inner Critic expressing its concerns and criticisms. Then, write a response letter from your Inner Warrior, addressing each point with compassion, support, and constructive solutions. This exercise may help you better articulate the perspectives of both voices and find a balanced approach.

As you get more accustomed to recognizing your triggers and you hear your Inner Critic, make a conscious effort to balance its feedback with positive reinforcement from your Inner Warrior. For instance, if your Inner Critic points out a mistake, let your Inner Warrior acknowledge the effort you put in, and remind you of your ability to learn and grow. An open, constructive dialogue between your Inner Critic and Inner Warrior allows both voices to contribute to your personal development in a balanced and constructive way.

Daily Mindful Self-Reflection

Daily mindful self-reflection is another powerful practice for maintaining a balanced relationship between your Inner Critic and Inner Warrior. By regularly checking in with yourself, you can monitor your internal dialogue and make adjustments as needed. This allows you to become aware of when your Inner Critic is becoming too vocal or when your Inner Warrior needs additional support.

Here are some questions to guide your inner dialogue:

- *What thoughts have dominated my internal conversation today? Were they mainly critical or supportive?*

- *Has my Inner Critic influenced my actions or decisions recently? Was it constructive or overly harsh?*

- *In what ways has my Inner Warrior shown up for me today? How did it help me face challenges or stay motivated?*

- *Are there any specific situations where I felt the balance between my Inner Critic and Inner Warrior was off? What can I do to restore that balance?*

- *What are some positive affirmations or reminders I can use to strengthen my Inner Warrior moving forward?*

By reflecting on these questions regularly, you can be aware of your internal dialogue and ensure that both voices are contributing to your growth in a balanced way.

Daily habits can also help maintain a healthy balance between your Inner Critic and Inner Warrior. These practices serve as reminders to stay mindful of your internal dialogue throughout the day. Try starting your day by checking in with your Inner Warrior. Rather than dwell on the challenges or struggles you'll likely face, approach the day with newfound curiosity.

Ask yourself questions like:

- *What is one good thing that will happen to me today?*

- *What am I looking forward to?*

- *What will I learn today?*

- *What challenges will I overcome today?*

Anticipating positive events helps to *'prime your mind'* for positivity. It becomes easier to recognize good things when they happen and sets a constructive tone for the day, allowing your Inner Warrior to take the lead. Then, throughout the day, reflect on what you're grateful for. Focusing on gratitude helps promote a more balanced, positive outlook.

Likewise, before going to bed, take a few moments to reflect on your internal dialogue and think about the balance between your Inner Critic and Inner Warrior. Recall moments when your Inner Critic might have spoken in an overly harsh manner and remind yourself of your accomplishments and strengths. Consistency is key to embedding these habits into daily life. By making them a regular part of your routine, you create a more balanced internal dialogue over time.

Continuous Learning and Intentionality

To achieve long-term growth and self-mastery, it is critical to adopt a mindset of continuous learning. By accepting that perfection is simply unattainable, you allow yourself to focus on progress and personal development rather than on meeting unrealistic standards. This frame of mind develops resilience, adaptability, and a willingness to learn from your mistakes.

As you strive to maintain the delicate balance between your Inner Critic and Inner Warrior, it is also important to ensure that you are intentional. Intentionality is a guiding principle that keeps you focused on what you want to accomplish long-term and how you plan to see those plans through.

Start by writing a clear and concise statement of your intention. For example, *"I will balance my Inner Critic and Inner Warrior in a way that supports my long-term self-compassion and growth."*

Next, list the specific actions you will take to support this intention. For instance, *"I will practice mindfulness meditation three times a week,"* or *"I will engage in daily self-reflection and journaling."*

Determine how often you will revisit your intention, assess your progress, and maintain accountability. For example, *I will reflect on my progress at the end of each week on Friday."*)

Finally, be open to adjustment based on your reflection and experiences. For instance, *"If I notice my Inner Critic is becoming too harsh, I will increase my self-compassion exercises."*

In the next chapter, we will focus on embracing courage and resilience, building on the foundation of balance we introduced in this chapter. We will discuss how to build a courageous and resilient mindset to meet challenges with strength and determination.

Chapter 7
Building Courage and Resilience

"Courage is resistance to fear, mastery of fear - not absence of fear."

Mark Twain

Courage and resilience are essential for pursuing your goals with determination. But what does it really mean to embody these traits? While balancing your Inner Critic and Inner Warrior provides a solid foundation for self-growth, courage and resilience help you face adversity head-on and recover from setbacks with strength and grace.

In this chapter, we'll explore courage in more detail—how to take bold actions despite fear, standing firm in convictions amid obstacles, and showing resilience. These qualities will help you continue on your journey toward self-mastery.

The Interplay Between Courage and Resilience

As we have touched on in prior chapters, courage is the ability to confront fear, uncertainty, and challenges with confidence and resolve. It can mean taking bold action despite feeling afraid and pushing beyond your comfort zone to face difficult situations head-on.

Resilience is the capacity to recover quickly from difficulties and adapt to adversity, maintaining mental and emotional strength. People who are resilient bounce back after setbacks, undeterred, and learn from their experiences. Resilience helps you to maintain a positive outlook even when things do not go as planned.

Resilience, in turn, builds on courage. As you practice resilience, you strengthen your ability to act courageously. The more often you bounce back from difficulties, the more confident you become to face whatever comes your way. Together, courage and resilience create a cycle of growth and empowerment, helping you to overcome self-doubt, face your Inner Critic, and strengthen your Inner Warrior.

Courage isn't just displaying grand acts of heroism. Most commonly, it shows up in small, everyday decisions and actions. These can be as simple as speaking up in front of others when you have a different perspective, trying new food from a different culture, or making a life change despite uncertainty. Demonstrating small acts of bravery is important because they push you outside your comfort zone and force you to confront your fears.

Over time, small acts of courage accumulate. Each courageous act proves that you are capable of handling greater levels of fear and uncertainty. This, in turn, reinforces inner strength and resilience, gradually diminishing self-doubt and nurturing your Inner Warrior.

The relationship between fear and courage can be understood as what some refer to as the *"fear-courage cycle."* When you confront fear head-on rather than avoiding it, this mere act reduces its power over you. The more you engage in this process, the less intimidating your fears become.

Building Resilience Despite Challenges

Resilience is not something we're born with; it is a skill that must be honed and strengthened over time. Everyone has the capacity to build resilience, but it grows only through practice and experience. Developing resilience involves seeing challenges as opportunities for growth rather than insurmountable obstacles.

Recovering from setbacks and failures is a process that involves learning from experiences and adapting to new circumstances. When experiencing setbacks, try the following approach:

First, acknowledge and accept your emotions. It's okay to feel disappointed, frustrated, or despondent after experiencing a setback. Recognizing these feelings allows you to process them rather than suppress them, which is vital for emotional healing.

Once you've acknowledged your emotions, take time to reflect on what happened. Consider what you can learn from the experience and how it might help you grow. Ask yourself: *What went well? What didn't go so well?* and *What could you do differently next time?* This reflection frames the problem as a valuable lesson.

After reflecting, create a game plan for moving forward. Identify at least three specific actions you can take to apply what you've learned and prevent similar setbacks in the future. This helps you regain a sense of control and purpose.

Strengthening Resilience Over Time

Strengthening resilience requires developing the right mindset, practicing self-compassion, and honing the skills that enable you to handle challenges effectively. Let's explore three key strategies for building resilience, starting with a growth mindset.

A growth mindset is the belief that your abilities and intelligence can be developed through effort, learning, and perseverance. This concept, popularized by psychologist Carol Dweck, is the opposite of a fixed mindset, where abilities are viewed as static and unchangeable. Embracing a growth mindset encourages you to see challenges as opportunities for development rather than threats to your self-worth.

By adopting a growth mindset, you direct your focus to learning, growth, and improvement. This perspective builds resilience by helping you view setbacks as valuable lessons for long-term growth.

For example, instead of thinking, *"I'm not good at this,"* someone with a growth mindset would say, *"I'm not good at this yet, but I'm going to improve with practice."* This subtle shift in thinking helps build resilience by reducing fear of failure and promoting a positive approach to challenges.

To start, monitor your self-talk and recognize when you might be limiting yourself with fixed beliefs. Challenge any negative thoughts you might be experiencing by reminding yourself that only effort and learning make growth possible. Recall past experiences where you've overcome a significant obstacle or learned a new skill, remembering that you can continue to grow and adapt.

The Importance of Problem-Solving Skills

Problem-solving is an essential life skill, vital for building resilience. When facing adversity, the ability to successfully identify a problem, generate solutions, and take action significantly affects how you manage the situation and move forward.

To develop your problem-solving skills, it's generally helpful to follow a structured approach. Start by clearly identifying the problem you're trying to solve. Take the necessary time to dissect the core issue and understand its root causes. Next, brainstorm possible solutions without immediately judging or dismissing any ideas that come to mind. Finally, decide on a solution. This approach helps you explore a variety of options and creative solutions.

Why Vulnerability is One of Your Greatest Strengths

From a young age, we are conditioned to see vulnerability as a sign of weakness, especially as men. We're taught to believe that showing vulnerability means exposing our flaws and opening ourselves up to criticism or rejection. But it's important to realize that vulnerability is actually a profound source of strength and courage.

Embracing vulnerability means being open and honest about your feelings, fears, and uncertainties, which requires immense bravery. It's allows others to see you as you truly are, without hiding behind a facade of success or perfection.

Viewing vulnerability as a strength allows you to create authentic connections, building trust and deepening relationships that encourage others to do the same. Vulnerability also supports your personal growth by pushing you beyond your comfort zone, taking risks, and confronting fears, all vital for resilience and personal achievement.

Changing your view of what vulnerability means leads to courageous actions that strengthen resilience. Being vulnerable means that you're more likely to take risks in pursuit of your goals, knowing that even if you fail, you had the courage to try.

For instance, asking for help when you're struggling is an act of vulnerability that can open doors to new opportunities and support. Sharing your true feelings with someone, even when it's uncomfortable, is another path to stronger, more meaningful relationships.

To embody these principles, start by being honest with yourself about your emotions and experiences. When you feel scared, uncertain, or insecure, acknowledge these feelings without judgment. Share your authentic self with others, whether by expressing your true thoughts and feelings, seeking support, or admitting when you don't have all the answers.

Building Resilience Through Authenticity

Closely connected to vulnerability is authenticity—being true to yourself and aligning your actions with your values. Authenticity, although often understated, is a key component of resilience. True authenticity reduces internal conflict and promotes inner peace, because you live a life that feels genuine and true to who you really are. When you are authentic, you are less likely to be swayed by external pressures or the opinions of others, which helps you stay grounded and resilient despite challenges.

To develop authenticity, start by clarifying your core values, *i.e.*, what matters most. This requires that you know who you are. Reflect and prioritize what is most important to you, and which principles guide your daily decisions and actions. Use this clarity to assess how well your current life aligns with your values and where there may be gaps.

Mindful living is another way to build authenticity and resilience. By being present in each moment and paying close attention to your thoughts, feelings, and actions, you can make conscious decisions that align with your true self. This helps you stay connected to your values and maintain a strong sense of self, even when facing external pressures or inevitable challenges.

Embracing vulnerability and authenticity enriches your life, builds deeper connections, greater self-awareness, and adds purpose. By living openly and authentically, you face life's problems with courage and confidence, knowing that you are true to yourself come what may.

Maintaining Courage and Resilience

Maintaining courage and resilience is an ongoing process. So it's important to have a long-term perspective. The growth process naturally involves both success and setbacks. There will be times when you feel strong and confident, and other times when you may struggle. Understanding that helps you stay committed to your path, even when progress feels slow.

Trust in your ability to grow and change over time, and be patient with yourself as you navigate this journey. Remember that each step, no matter how small, contributes to your overall development and strengthens your Inner Warrior. Stay focused on your long-term goals, but also appreciate the progress you make along the way.

Continuously remind yourself that these qualities are like muscles that grow stronger with use. The more resilient you are in recovering from setbacks, the more courageous you become. Keep a positive outlook and stay committed to your journey, trusting that your efforts will lead to lasting change and self-mastery.

By maintaining a long-term perspective, you sustain your courage and resilience over time. This helps you stay grounded, motivated, and empowered, helping you face life with continued confidence and determination.

The Path to Self-Mastery

Self-mastery is the ultimate goal of personal growth. This happens when you harmoniously balance your Inner Critic and Inner Warrior. It is the process of gaining control over your thoughts, emotions, and actions to live a life that aligns with your values and aspirations. Achieving self-mastery means developing a deep understanding of yourself and cultivating the ability to respond to life's challenges with wisdom, courage, and a sense of composure.

As you work towards self-mastery, you learn to manage your Inner Critic constructively, using it as a tool for growth rather than allowing it to dominate your thoughts and undermine your confidence. At the same time, you strengthen your Inner Warrior to the point where you feel empowered to face fears, take risks, and bounce back from setbacks. This balance between self-reflection and self-empowerment forms the foundation for a complete and fulfilling life.

In the next chapter, we will explore the journey to self-mastery in more depth. We'll look at the practices and habits that support long-term growth and self-discovery, helping you to continue developing your inner strength and resilience. As you prepare for this journey, remember that the primary focus of self-mastery is continuous growth and learning, not perfection. It is a path that requires patience, dedication, and a commitment to living authentically and courageously.

Chapter 8
The Journey Toward Self-Mastery

"Mastering oneself is true power"

Lao Tzu

The journey toward self-mastery is a lifelong endeavor of growth, learning, and self-discovery. It means becoming the best version of yourself, not by achieving perfection, but by continually striving to understand and improve who you are. Self-mastery requires balance between your Inner Critic with your Inner Warrior, as well as embracing courage, and developing resilience. It means cultivating the habits, mindsets, and practices that allow you to live a life aligned with your values and goals.

In this chapter, we will explore self-mastery and how to cultivate it in your life. We'll discuss the importance of self-awareness, discipline, and intentionality in guiding your actions and decisions. You will learn strategies for building skills and habits that support long-term growth and self-empowerment.

The 3 Pillars of Self-Mastery

Self-mastery is the continuous process of gaining control over your thoughts, emotions, and behaviors so that you can live in alignment with your values and goals. It means understanding who you are at your core, recognizing your strengths and weaknesses, and making conscious choices that reflect your true self.

Self-mastery is supported by three fundamental pillars: self-awareness, self-discipline, and self-compassion. They provide the foundation for long-term growth, self-empowerment, and well-being. Each contributes in a unique way to becoming the best version of yourself.

Pillar 1: Self-Awareness.

Self-awareness is the ability to observe and understand your own thoughts, emotions, and behaviors the way others do. It involves recognizing your patterns, triggers, and motivations, and using this knowledge and insight to make conscious decisions that align with your values and goals. Self-awareness is the first step toward self-mastery because it helps you identify the areas where you want to grow and change.

Pillar 2: Self-Discipline.

Self-discipline means exercising control over your impulses and maintaining focus on your long-term goals. It requires that you resist short-term temptations and stay committed to your chosen path, even when it is difficult. Self-discipline is essential for self-mastery because it helps you build the habits and behaviors that support your growth and align with your values.

Pillar 3: Self-Compassion.

Self-compassion involves treating yourself with kindness and understanding, especially during times of intense struggle or failure. It means acknowledging your imperfections and giving yourself a measure of grace. Self-compassion is vital for self-mastery because it helps you bounce back quickly from setbacks, and encourages a positive and supportive relationship with yourself.

Together, these three pillars of self-mastery work together to help you grow, adapt, and thrive. By cultivating self-awareness, self-discipline, and self-compassion, you can live a life that is true to your values and goals, ultimately achieving greater fulfillment and purpose.

Self-Awareness and Self-Mastery

Self-awareness plays a vital role in understanding how your thoughts, emotions, and behaviors influence your personal growth and relationships. By being aware of your internal state, you can recognize the patterns that shape your actions and the triggers that result in strong emotional responses. This allows you to make conscious choices, rather than being driven by automatic reactions or ingrained habits.

Additionally, self-awareness helps you identify areas where you might want to grow or change. For instance, if you notice that you often react defensively in certain situations, becoming aware of this pattern allows you to explore its roots and work on responding more constructively. [1] Similarly, understanding your natural talents, strengths and areas of comfort can guide you in making decisions that leverage these attributes while challenging yourself to step out of your comfort zone and develop new skills.

How to Cultivate Self-Awareness

Self-awareness requires intentional practice and reflection. Here are some practical ways to cultivate greater self-awareness:

Mindfulness involves paying attention to the present moment without judging the thoughts and emotions you feel. By practicing mindfulness, you can become more attuned to your thoughts and feelings as they arise, calmly noticing them without immediately reacting. This heightened awareness allows

---

1. It's important to point out that sometimes this process cannot be done in isolation. Seeking the help of a trained mental health professional can support your progress better than relying on your own efforts.

you to observe your internal experiences more clearly and understand how they influence your behavior.

Journaling is another powerful tool for self-reflection and self-awareness. By regularly writing about your experiences, thoughts, and emotions you feel, you can gain deeper insights into your patterns and triggers. Journaling provides a safe, open space for honest self-exploration, helping you reveal the underlying beliefs and motivations that shape your actions.

Sometimes, others can see aspects of ourselves that we may overlook. Receiving guidance and feedback from trusted friends, family members, or colleagues can provide valuable insights on how your behaviors and attitudes impact those around you. Being open to constructive feedback allows you to better understand yourself and identify areas for growth.

Practice these activities regularly. Set aside time for mindfulness exercises, write in your journal consistently, and actively seek feedback from those you trust. Over time, they will help you develop a clearer, more nuanced understanding of yourself.

Overcoming Resistance to Self-Awareness

Despite its importance, cultivating self-awareness can often be a challenge. Internal barriers such as defensiveness, denial, and a fear of facing harsh or uncomfortable truths may impede your progress. These obstacles can prevent us from acknowledging certain aspects of our personality and hinder personal growth.

Begin by approaching self-awareness with a compassionate mindset. Understand that everyone, including you, has flaws and areas for improvement. So, be gentle with yourself as you focus on your journey of self-mastery. Self-compassion reduces the fear of facing uncomfortable truths by creating a safe space for honest self-reflection.

Embrace curiosity and openness when reflecting on your thoughts, emotions, and behavior. Instead of immediately dismissing feedback or resisting others' observations, try to see them as opportunities for growth. Keeping an open mind allows you to learn more about yourself and adapt to new insights.

Finally, look at your vulnerability as a hidden strength, recognizing that being open to self-exploration is a courageous act that relatively few pursue with any level of seriousness. The path to self-awareness requires facing aspects of yourself that may be uncomfortable or challenging. By accepting our vulnerabilities at face value, we create room for growth and self-improvement.

By addressing these barriers, you enhance your self-awareness and move closer to achieving self-mastery. As you become more aware of your inner experiences, you gain the ability to make more intentional choices, and lead a more fulfilling life.

Developing Self-Discipline

Self-discipline carries a negative connotation in society, but it is a powerful concept and an essential life skill for success. It is the ability to regulate your own thoughts, emotions, and behaviors to pursue long-term goals, despite short-term temptations or distractions. It requires you to stay focused on what truly matters, resisting the urge to indulge in immediate gratification that may derail your progress.

Remember, self-discipline is not rigid self-control. Rather, it involves making choices that align with your values and aspirations, even when they require effort, sacrifice and perseverance. The role of self-discipline in personal and professional success cannot be overstated. It is a key factor in building resilience, because it helps maintain your commitment to your goals despite setbacks or difficulties.

Self-discipline also enables you to suppress the voice of your Inner Critic and amplify the voice of your Inner Warrior. While the Inner Critic may tempt you to just give up when things get tough, the Inner Warrior provides the courage and inspiration to keep going. By harmonizing these voices, self-discipline allows you to achieve your objectives while maintaining a healthy sense of self-worth and determination.

Strengthening Your Self-Discipline

Developing self-discipline requires clear intention, structured planning, and dedication. Here are some ways to help you build and strengthen your self-discipline:

Begin by creating specific, measurable, and achievable goals that align with your long-term values and aspirations. Having clear and intentional life goals give you a sense of direction and purpose, making it easier to stay disciplined.

Develop routines that support your goals and reduce the need for constant decision-making. Having a structured routine will help you establish healthy habits, making it easier to stay disciplined over time. For example, setting a regular schedule for exercise or dedicating specific times each day for focused work can help build self-discipline.

Most importantly, train yourself to delay immediate rewards in favor of long-term benefits. This practice strengthens your ability to resist short-term temptations and stay committed to your goals. Start with small tasks, like waiting 24 hours before making an impulse purchase, and gradually build up to more challenging tasks.

Break large tasks into smaller, manageable steps to stay motivated and to prevent feeling overwhelmed. Tracking your progress over time can also provide a sense of accomplishment and help you to keep going. Rewarding yourself for reaching milestones also reinforces your commitment and inspires you to keep going.

Overcoming Challenges to Self-Discipline

While self-discipline is crucial for success, maintaining it is definitely not easy. Common challenges include procrastination, distractions, and lack of motivation, which can quickly undermine your efforts to stay on track.

Begin by setting clear boundaries to minimize distractions and create a conducive environment for focus and productivity. This might involve setting specific times for work and rest, limiting social media usage, or creating a dedicated workspace that minimizes distractions and interruptions.

Additionally, be sure to manage your time effectively by utilizing time management techniques, such as the Pomodoro Technique or Time Blocking to structure your day and prioritize tasks. Time management helps you allocate enough time for meaningful activities and also reduces the likelihood of procrastination.

Remember that self-discipline is a skill that can be cultivated with practice, patience, and persistence. These practices lead to lasting growth and fulfillment as you continue on your journey to self-mastery.

The Role of Self-Compassion in Self-Mastery

Self-compassion is vital to emotional well-being, resilience, and a positive self-image. It involves treating yourself with the same kindness, understanding, and care you would extend to a close friend. In the journey toward self-mastery, self-compassion is a powerful buffer against your Inner Critic, allowing you to handle setbacks and challenges with grace instead of self-criticism.

Interestingly, we often tend to treat others much better than we treat ourselves. From a tender age, we are taught to treat colleagues, family and close friends with kindness, empathy and respect. However, we are rarely given the instruction and guidance to extend ourselves the same courtesy.

Self-compassion creates a supportive internal environment that builds resilience. Instead of berating yourself for mistakes, you acknowledge your humanity and the inevitability of flaws. This compassionate approach views setbacks simply as another life lesson. A new opportunity for learning and development—not evidence of inadequacy.

To start, pay attention to your inner dialogue, especially during difficult times. Practice speaking to yourself with the same kindness and encouragement you would offer to a friend. For example, instead of saying, *"I can't believe I messed up,"* try saying, *"It's okay to make mistakes. I'm learning and growing from this experience."*

Likewise, when you feel negative emotions (and we all have them), allow yourself to feel them without labeling them as good or bad. Recognize that emotions are a natural part of the human experience and feeling sad, frustrated, or disappointed is okay. This non-judgmental self-acceptance helps you process your emotions and reduces the tendency to suppress or ignore them.

Another key aspect of self-compassion is caring for your physical, emotional, and mental health. Your Inner Warrior can only thrive when you regularly engage in activities that nourish your body, mind, and spirit, such as exercise, meditation, hobbies, or simply spending time in nature. Self-care is not indulgent or selfish; it's a necessary practice that supports your overall health and resilience.

Consistency is essential to integrating self-compassion into your life. By r making self-compassion a regular part of your daily routine, you create a foundation of emotional resilience and self-acceptance. This compassionate approach to self-mastery empowers you to navigate life's challenges with greater ease and confidence.

Reflecting on Your Growth and Progress

Periodic reflection is another vital practice in your journey to self-mastery. It allows you to assess your growth, recognize incremental achievements, and identify new areas for improvement. Reflecting regularly creates an internal headspace for seeing just how far you have come and what steps you should take next. This keeps you aligned with your goals and values, so your actions continue supporting your long-term vision.

Reflection also keeps you motivated. When you take time to periodically review your progress, you can see the tangible results of your efforts, which reinforces your commitment to your journey. Reflection and journaling can provide structure, helping you dive deeper into your experiences and draw meaningful insights.

For instance:

- *What have I learned about myself in the past week or month?*

- *Which actions or decisions have brought me closer to my goals?*

- *What challenges have I faced, and how have I responded to them?*

- *Where do I see opportunities for further growth or improvement?*

Every attempt to reach a goal, whether successful or not, offers valuable lessons that contribute to your ongoing growth and development. Reflection helps you to view both positive and negative outcomes as opportunities for learning. This mindset shift changes temporary setbacks into stepping stones, so that you approach new problems with curiosity rather than fear.

Learning from experiences involves taking the time to understand what worked well and what didn't, then extract the underlying lessons and apply them to future situations. It means that you acknowledge that mistakes and failures are not reflections of your worth, but rather integral parts of the learning process. This perspective builds resilience, as each challenge faced and overcome strengthens your Inner Warrior and prepares you for the next challenge.

Make it a habit to ask yourself the following questions:

- *What did I learn from this experience?*

- *How can I use this knowledge to improve and grow?*

- *What strengths did I demonstrate, and how can I leverage them moving forward?*

- *What could I do differently next time to achieve a better outcome?*

Embracing Self-Mastery as a Lifelong Process

It's important to remember that self-mastery is not a single destination in life. It's a lifelong journey of growth, learning, and adaptation. It involves continually refining the understanding of yourself, adjusting your goals, and then evolving in response to new experiences and challenges.

You must stay committed to the journey, recognizing that the path to self-mastery will continue to evolve with life's changes and challenges. Realize that every stage of life brings new lessons and opportunities for growth. Some phases might require that you focus on building resilience and courage, while others might need a greater emphasis on self-compassion and reflection. Viewing the process as ongoing allows you to remain open to growth and transformation, no matter where you are on your path.

As you continue to progress in your journey, it's important to periodically reflect from time to time on your existing goals, refine them, and set new goals that reflect your current values and aspirations. This practice keeps you engaged and focused on personal growth and self-empowerment, ensuring that you continue to evolve and grow over time.

Reflect on what matters most to you at this current stage in your life. Ask yourself: *"In which areas of life do I want to improve?" "What skills do I want to develop?"* and *"What new experiences you I want to embrace?"* Use the answers to these questions to create specific, measurable, and achievable goals that align with your long-term values and vision for your life.

Seeking Feedback and Accountability

Asking for feedback and seeking accountability is another important aspect of self-mastery. Feedback from others provides a fresh perspective on your progress, helping you identify areas for improvement and keeping you focused on your goals. Accountability partners, whether friends, mental health professionals, mentors, or coaches, can also support this process by offering encouragement, monitoring your progress, and holding you responsible for honoring the commitments you make to yourself.

When requesting feedback, ask for specific input rather than general comments. For example, you might ask, *"What do you think I could improve in my approach to handling stress?"* or *"How did my presentation come across to you?"* Genuinely listen, and be open to different perspectives, even if they are difficult to hear. Constructive feedback is designed to help you grow, and being receptive to it is a sign of strength and maturity.

Own Your Power. Shape Your Destiny.

As you continue your journey toward self-mastery, do so confidently and purposefully. Trust in your ability to navigate life's challenges and achieve your goals. You are enough—you have the tools, insights, and strength within you to create a life that aligns with your values, aspirations, and true potential.

Commit to this path with all your heart. Face your fears, challenge your limits, and push beyond the boundaries of what you once thought possible. Remember, the journey to self-mastery is a lifelong adventure, rich with opportunities for transformation and fulfillment. Take the first step today, and continue moving forward with the knowledge that you can achieve greatness.

You have the power to shape your own destiny. By embracing courage, resilience, and self-belief, you will make choices that reflect your true potential and create a life of purpose and fulfillment. Remember, the future is not something that happens to you—it is something you create starting with the actions you take today.

Remember, empowered action is the bridge between intention and reality. Take that first step with confidence, knowing that you have the tools, insights, and inner strength to achieve your goals. As you move forward, trust in your ability to overcome challenges, silence self-doubt, and live a life that reflects your true potential.

Hopefully, reading this book has helped you in some small way to prepare you for this moment—now it's time to step into your power and make it happen!

Thank you for the opportunity to be a part of your journey!

With Love and Gratitude,

Donovan Garett

Where to Find Help

If you (or someone you care about) is in need of help, here is a list of agencies dedicated to providing free mental health support in the United States, Canada, the United Kingdom, and Mexico:

United States

National Suicide Prevention Lifeline: 24/7 free and confidential support for people in distress, prevention, and crisis resources.

- **Website**: suicidepreventionlifeline.org

- **Phone**: 1-800-273-TALK (8255) or 988 (crisis line)

SAMHSA's (Substance Abuse and Mental Health Services Administration) National Helpline: Free, confidential, 24/7 treatment referral and information service for individuals and families facing mental and/or substance use disorders.

- **Website**: samhsa.gov/find-help/national-helpline

- **Phone**: 1-800-662-HELP (4357)

Mental Health America (MHA): Advocacy, education, research, and support for mental health conditions; provides a range of resources and local support services.

- **Website**: mhanational.org

Crisis Text Line: Free, 24/7 text-based mental health support.

- **Website**: crisistextline.org
- **Text**: Text HOME to 741741

NAMI (National Alliance on Mental Illness)

1. **Services**: Free education, advocacy, and support groups for individuals with mental health conditions and their families.
2. **Website**: nami.org

Canada

Kids Help Phone: 24/7 free and confidential mental health support for young people in Canada.

- **Website**: kidshelpphone.ca
- **Phone**: 1-800-668-6868

- **Text**: Text CONNECT to 686868

Canadian Mental Health Association (CMHA): Mental health programs and services, public education, advocacy, and resources.

- **Website**: cmha.ca

Wellness Together Canada: Free mental health and substance use support, including one-on-one counseling.

- **Website**: https://wellnesstogether.ca/

- **Phone**: 1-866-585-0445

Crisis Services Canada: National network for suicide prevention and crisis intervention.

- **Website**: crisisservicescanada.ca / https://988.ca/

- **Phone**: 1-833-456-4566

- **Text**: Text 45645

- **Call or Text 9-8-8**

Indigenous Services Canada – Hope for Wellness Help Line: Immediate mental health counseling and crisis intervention to all Indigenous peoples across Canada.

- **Website**: hopeforwellness.ca

- **Phone**: 1-855-242-3310

United Kingdom

Samaritans: 24/7 free support for anyone in emotional distress or struggling to cope.

- **Website**: samaritans.org

- **Phone**: 116 123

Mind: Information, support, and advice for people experiencing mental health problems.

- **Website**: mind.org.uk

Rethink Mental Illness: Advocacy, support groups, and services for people affected by mental illness.

- **Website**: rethink.org

- **Phone**: 0300 5000 927

Shout: 24/7 text messaging service providing free mental health support.

- **Website**: giveusashout.org

- **Text**: Text SHOUT to 85258

The Mix: Free support and counseling for young people under 25.

- **Website**: themix.org.uk

- **Phone**: 0808 808 4994

Mexico

Línea de la Vida (National Mental Health Hotline): 24/7 mental health support and crisis intervention.

1. **Website**: gob.mx/salud

2. **Phone**: 800 911 2000

SAPTEL (Sistema de Atención Psicológica por Teléfono): Free psychological counseling via phone, available 24/7.

1. **Phone**: 55 5259 8121

Frente Nacional para la Sororidad: Support for women in abusive relationships and those experiencing psychological distress.

1. **Website**: frentenacional.mx

Centro de Integración Juvenil (CIJ): Mental health services focused on prevention and treatment of substance use disorders, including psychological counseling.

1. **Website:** https://www.gob.mx/salud/cij

2. **Phone:** 55 5212 1212

Mexican Red Cross – Psychological Support Services: Psychological support for individuals in crisis or affected by traumatic events.

1. **Website:** cruzrojamexicana.org.mx

2. **Phone:** 55 1084 9000

Let's Connect!

If you enjoyed this book, I'd love to keep the conversation going. Join my mailing list for member-only insights, tips to help you grow your business, enhance your leadership skills, and achieve your personal and professional goals. You'll also get updates on new books and projects (and a few freebies here and there).

Sign up today and take the next step on your journey!

Click or Scan:

Love FREE Books?
Join our Advance Reader Copy Program!

Do you love new books and sharing your thoughts with others? I'm looking for passionate readers to join my **Advance Reader Copy (ARC) program**!

As a member, you'll get **FREE early access** to my latest books before they're officially released. In return, all I ask is that you share an honest review on one (or more) platforms, helping other readers discover my work.

Click or scan below to learn more:

Your feedback means the world to me, and I can't wait to share my next book with you!

www.ingramcontent.com/pod-product-compliance
Lightning Source LLC
LaVergne TN
LVHW011208080426
835508LV00007B/664